THE POWER OF HABIT

George Duhigg

THE POWER OF HABIT

The 7 habits of the world's most efficient people

Avenet Edition

Copyright © 2023 - Avenet Edition

All rights reserved. No part of this publication may be reproduced, distributed or transmitted in any form or by any means, including photocopying, recording or other electronic or mechanical methods, without the prior written permission of the publisher, except in the case of brief quotations incorporated in reviews and certain other non-commercial uses permitted by copyright law. All references to historical events, real people or places may be real or used fictitiously to respect anonymity. Names, characters and places may be the product of the author's imagination.

Disclaimer :

The information contained in this book is for educational and informational purposes only. The author and publisher do not guarantee that the strategies described will produce results for all readers. It is important to understand that results depend on many factors such as industry, competition, economics and other external factors. Consequently, neither the author nor the publisher can be held responsible for any damage or loss suffered in connection with the application of the information contained in this book.

Contents

FOREWORD 9

THE POWER OF HABITS 13

FORGING DESTINY THROUGH HABIT...................................... 13
THE GOOD, THE BAD AND THE USUAL 15
THE WHEELS OF SUCCESS 17
THE DANCE OF THE NEURONS - UNDERSTANDING THE PSYCHOLOGY OF HABITS 19
THE SEVEN PILLARS OF SUCCESS: MAKING AN INFORMED CHOICE 23

HABIT #1 - START WITH THE END IN SIGHT 27

ARCHITECTE DE SA VIE : DEFINIR OBJECTIFS ET VISION.............. 27
THE POWER OF LONG-TERM VISION 30
VISION WORKSHOP: DESIGN YOUR FUTURE 31
WHEN DREAMS BECOME REALITY 33

HABIT #2 - MANAGING YOUR TIME - PUTTING PRIORITIES FIRST....................................... 39

URGENT VS IMPORTANT : THE EFFICIENCY COMPASS 39

THE MAGIC OF 80/20: THE SECRET OF PRIORITIES.................43
MASTER OF TIME: THE ART OF ORGANIZATION 47
THE ANTI-PROCRASTINATION SHIELD...................................51

HABIT #3 - BE PROACTIVE...55

CAPTAINING YOUR SHIP: THE NATURE OF PROACTIVITY 55
FORGING PROACTIVITY...58
FROM IDEA TO ACTION: THE STORY OF EFFICIENCY 60
SURVIVAL KIT FOR THE PROACTIVE 63

HABIT #4 - SEEK TO UNDERSTAND, THEN TO BE UNDERSTOOD..65

THE GIFT OF LISTENING: THE IMPORTANCE OF ACTIVE LISTENING 65
AMPLIFICATEUR DE COMMUNICATION : AMELIORER SES COMPETENCES 67
THE POWER OF UNDERSTANDING: INSPIRING ANECDOTES 70

HABIT #5 - THINK WIN-WIN...73

BEYOND COMPETITION: THE HARMONY OF COOPERATION 73
VALUE CREATOR: BUILDING MUTUALLY BENEFICIAL RELATIONSHIPS 76
PACIFIC NEGOTIATOR: CONFLICT RESOLUTION STRATEGIES 78
THE ROAD TO WIN-WIN: SUCCESS STORIES 81

HABIT #6 - SELF-DISCIPLINE: THE SECRET OF CONSISTENCY 85

CONSISTENCY IN EFFORT: THE KEY TO SUCCESS 85
THE PILLARS OF SELF-DISCIPLINE: STRATEGIES AND TECHNIQUES 88
BUILDING A SUCCESS ROUTINE: EXERCISES AND ACTION PLANS . 90
STORIES OF SELF-DISCIPLINE: LESSONS FROM THE WINNERS 92

HABIT #7 - SHARPEN THE SAW 97

THE SPIRIT GARDENER: THE IMPORTANCE OF CONTINUOUS SELF-IMPROVEMENT 97
THE MOTIVATION MARATHON: STAY FOCUSED ON PERSONAL GROWTH 100
PERSONAL DEVELOPMENT TOOLBOX 102
FROM CATERPILLAR TO BUTTERFLY: STORIES OF TRANSFORMATION 104

LE FIL ROUGE: SUMMARY OF THE 7 HABITS 109

BEYOND THE BOOK: CONCLUSION 113

APPENDICES 117
SOURCE IMAGES 120

FOREWORD

Dear readers,

Welcome to this adventure. If you're holding this book in your hands or reading these words on a screen, it means you're ready to explore your potential, to develop powerful habits that can transform your life. It's a bold first step, and I'm honored to be your guide on this exciting quest.

Allow me to introduce myself. My name is George Duhigg. I'm a passionate entrepreneur and trainer of effective habits. I've dedicated much of my life to understanding and studying how small actions, repeated day after day, can have a colossal impact on our lives. Through my personal and professional experiences, I've discovered that effectiveness isn't just about being productive at work or achieving business goals. It also encompasses our personal well-being, life satisfaction and the quality of our relationships.

From my own experience, I can tell you that it's not always easy to become aware of the habits that govern us. Some are deeply rooted, formed over years, even decades. They can be so pervasive that we no longer even recognize them as habits, but simply as "the way we do things". However, by taking the time to examine these repetitive behaviors and attitudes, we can begin to see how they shape our lives, for better or worse.

My passion is not limited to understanding these principles. What really fascinates me is helping others apply them in their daily lives. I've had the privilege of working with many individuals and organizations, helping them discover their potential and unlock their effectiveness by reformulating their habits.

I want to share these discoveries with you. I don't claim to have all the answers, and this book doesn't promise a quick fix to all your problems. But what I can offer is a collection of principles and strategies that I've found to be effective, backed up by research, anecdotes and personal experience.

This book is for anyone looking to improve their effectiveness, whether you're an aspiring entrepreneur, an established professional looking to evolve, a student trying to find your way, or simply someone who wants to live a more rewarding and satisfying life. There are no prerequisites, other than an open mind and a willingness to learn and grow.

I'm excited to start this journey with you and can't wait to see where it takes us.

Onwards and upwards!

Your opinion counts!

Once you've finished this book, share your review on Amazon.

Your feedback will be useful for future readers.

I look forward to seeing how this book has impacted you.

Thank you in advance for your contribution, and happy reading!

THE REAL POWER OF HABITS

Forging Destiny Through Habit

In the hustle and bustle of our modern lives, it can be easy to forget that each day is made up of thousands of moments, each offering us the opportunity to make a choice. Every decision, no matter how insignificant, is a stone we add to the edifice of our existence. Each choice forges a part of our path, and over time, these decisions accumulate and become what we call habits. But how important are these habits in shaping our daily lives? How do they shape our existence? To begin answering these questions, we first need to understand what habits are.

A habit is a routine of behavior that is repeated regularly and tends to occur subconsciously. It's like a program that our brain runs automatically without us having to think about it consciously. Habits can be as simple as brushing your teeth every morning or as complex as an athlete's routine before a competition.

Our habits largely define our daily lives. They determine the way we get up in the morning, the way we dress, the way we work, and even the way we interact with others. Habits are the foundation on which we build our daily lives.

Habit formation can be an incredibly powerful tool to help us achieve our goals and live the life we want. Well-established habits act as shortcuts that our brains use to perform tasks more efficiently. Instead of spending energy thinking about every little decision, we can use that energy to focus on more important tasks. This can free up huge amounts of time and energy that we can devote to more productive tasks.

However, not all habits are beneficial. Some habits, like smoking or spending too much time on social networks, can be detrimental to our health and well-being. These bad habits can hold us back, preventing us from achieving our goals and living the life we want. That's why it's essential to be aware of our habits and actively work to improve them. These bad habits are sometimes particularly hard to break, but we'll understand later why a habit is so hard to break.

But how do habits shape our existence? Each habit we form is like a thread in the tapestry of our lives. Each thread contributes to the color and texture of our existence. Some habits can help us weave a life of health, happiness and success, while others can contribute to a life of stress, frustration and failure.

Habits are the means by which we translate our thoughts, values and aspirations into real action. They are the link between what we think and what we do. For example, if we believe in the power of hard work and perseverance, we are likely to develop habits of diligence and resilience. Similarly, if we value health and well-being, we're likely to form habits of regular exercise and eating well. In this way, our habits reflect our beliefs and values and serve as a vehicle for realizing our aspirations.

It's essential to note that, although habits are powerful, they are not set in stone. They are malleable and can be modified with time and effort. We can choose to reinforce beneficial habits and break harmful ones. This process of changing habits can be difficult and requires patience and perseverance, but it is entirely possible and can have a profound impact on our lives.

Our habits have a direct and significant impact on the quality of our lives. They determine how we spend our time, how we interact with others, and ultimately how we feel in our daily lives. Habits influence not only our personal and professional effectiveness, but also our happiness and life satisfaction.

By understanding the fundamental role that habits play in our lives, we can begin to use them to our advantage. We can deliberately choose to form habits that help us achieve our goals and live the life we want. The ability to develop and maintain beneficial habits is one of the most important skills we can acquire.

It's time to recognize the power of habits and start using them to our advantage.

THE GOOD, THE BAD AND THE USUAL

In life, there are good habits, bad habits and those that are so deeply ingrained in our routine as to be almost invisible. Each of these categories has a significant impact on our personal and professional effectiveness. Let's take a moment to analyze how these habits affect our daily lives.

Let's start with good habits. These are like faithful friends who guide us to success. For example, a good habit of meticulous preparation can improve our professional efficiency by enabling us to be ready to face the challenges of the day. Similarly, a good habit of regular physical exercise can enhance our personal effectiveness by strengthening our overall health and well-being. These good habits are our allies, working behind the scenes to help us achieve our goals.

Let's move on to bad habits. They are like parasites that cling to us and hinder us. A bad habit of procrastination, for example, can seriously damage our professional efficiency by preventing us from completing tasks on time. A bad habit of compulsive snacking can affect our personal effectiveness by sabotaging our health and well-being. These bad habits are our enemies, acting underhand to derail us from our goals.

Finally, there are those habits so deeply ingrained that we consider them second nature. We call them "habitual" habits. They can be good or bad, but what sets them apart is their ability to operate under the radar of our consciousness. For example, a habitual habit of constantly checking our phone can reduce our professional efficiency by fragmenting our attention. On the other hand, a habitual habit of taking a few minutes each day to meditate can enhance our personal effectiveness by strengthening our mental and emotional balance. These habitual habits have the power to shape our lives, often without us even being aware of it.

It's essential to understand that all our habits, whether good, bad or habitual, have an impact on our effectiveness. They form the fabric of our daily lives and influence the way we act, think and feel. By recognizing and understanding the impact of these habits, we can take steps to reinforce the good ones, eradicate the bad ones, and make conscious changes to those that have become habitual. In this way, we can use our habits to shape a more effective and satisfying life.

The habits we cultivate largely define our lives. They are like tools we use constantly, often without even realizing it. For example, if you've got into the habit of getting up early every morning to do some sport, it can have far-reaching benefits for your overall health and well-being. You'll start the day with more energy, improve your physical condition and have a clearer mind to tackle the day's challenges. It's a habit that could be called "good" because it contributes to your personal effectiveness.

THE WHEELS OF SUCCESS

Habits are the silent cogs that propel the engine of our success. The positive habits we adopt are like the well-oiled parts of a gear that, day after day, bring us closer to our goals. To understand how this works, it's useful to take a closer look at the mechanisms of success.

Success, in any area of life, is rarely the result of an isolated event or a stroke of luck. Instead, success tends to be the product of continuous effort, sound decisions and small victories accumulated over time. In this context, our habits play a decisive role.

Let's take physical health as an example. If your goal is to get in shape, you probably won't get there with just one intense workout. On the contrary, it's the habit of exercising regularly, eating healthily and taking care of your rest that, together, will lead you towards your goal.

Similarly, in the professional realm, success isn't usually the result of a single great accomplishment. Instead, it's the habits of hard work, continuous learning, networking and effective time management that are most likely to lead you to the achievement of your career goals.

It's also important to note that developing beneficial habits can have a positive impact on several areas of your life simultaneously. For example, the habit of getting up early in the morning can not only give you more time to concentrate on your work, but also offer you a quiet moment for personal reflection or exercise, improving both your professional productivity and your personal well-being.

Let's remember that creating beneficial habits is a process that takes time and patience. It's not an overnight transformation, but a long-term commitment to positive change. However, every small victory, every beneficial habit you adopt, every positive change you make, is a step closer to your success.

The cogs of success are within you, in the form of your daily habits. By consciously shaping them to work in your favor, you can truly build the life of success you desire.

The Dance of Neurons - Understanding the Psychology of Habits

Let's delve into the intricacies of our mind, to discover how a habit is established. To do this, we must first understand that our brain is an extraordinarily efficient organ. It is constantly looking for ways to save energy. One of the ways it does this is by automating as many tasks as possible, in the form of habits.

The Habit Circuit

A habit, in the neurological sense, is an automated process that our brain has learned to minimize cognitive effort. Neuroscientist Daniel Kahneman summed up this concept in his book "Thinking, Fast and Slow", explaining that our brains operate on two systems. System 1 is fast, instinctive and emotional, while System 2 is slow, reflective and logical. Habits are firmly anchored in System 1.

When a habit is formed, a three-part cycle occurs: signal, routine and reward. The signal is a stimulus that triggers the routine, which is the action we perform repeatedly. The reward is what motivates us to repeat this action. To give a concrete example, let's say your phone rings (signal), you answer it (routine), and you take part in an interesting conversation (reward). This reward reinforces the routine, making it more likely that you'll respond in the same way to the same signal in the future.

However, not all signals lead to beneficial routines. A cue can also trigger a bad habit, as when stress (cue) drives you to snack (routine), which provides temporary relief (reward). By understanding this loop, you can begin to dismantle bad habits and build new, more beneficial ones.

Neuroplasticity: Sculpting the Brain

Let's move on to an equally fascinating concept: neuroplasticity. This is our brain's ability to reconfigure itself in response to our experiences. The brain is not a static organ, but a dynamic landscape that is constantly reshaped by our thoughts, actions and experiences.

When we perform an action for the first time, our brain creates a new neural pathway. It's like cutting a path through a virgin forest - the first time, it's difficult and requires a lot of effort. However, each time we repeat the action, this neural path becomes stronger. It's as if we're going over and over the same path in the forest, until it becomes a well-defined, easy-to-follow route. This is how habits are formed.

Neuroplasticity also means that we have the ability to change our habits. By performing new actions, we can create new neural pathways, and by stopping practicing old habits, old pathways can weaken. This gives a glimmer of hope to those struggling with stubborn habits - with time and perseverance, it's possible to reorganize neural pathways to support new, better habits.

21, 30, 66 days? Time to Form a Habit

There's a widely held belief that it takes 21 days to form a habit. This belief dates back to the plastic psychologist Dr Maxwell Maltz, who noted in the 1960s that his patients seemed to adapt to their new circumstances in around 21 days. However, this observation has been misinterpreted and generalized to all habits, whatever their complexity or context.

More recent studies have painted a more nuanced picture. A University College London study found that the time it takes to form a habit can vary considerably from person to person and habit to habit, ranging from 18 to 254 days, with an average of 66 days. The study also showed that regularity was more important than frequency - doing something every day, even a little, was more effective at forming a habit than doing a lot at once.

Ultimately, it's important to understand that habit formation is not a race, but a gradual march. Instead of focusing on the number of days, concentrate on regularity and patience. Your brain will adapt at its own pace.

The Role of Dopamine

Finally, we can't talk about the psychology of habits without mentioning dopamine, the neurotransmitter that plays a key role in our brain's reward circuit. When we receive a reward, our brain releases dopamine, giving us a feeling of pleasure. This is what makes us repeat the action that led to the reward. Dopamine is therefore a key element in the formation and maintenance of habits.

Dopamine can be released very easily, especially through bad habits. Smoking a cigarette, scrolling through TikTok or eating fast food all release large amounts of dopamine, which is why we continue to do these bad things. That's why it's so hard to "stop" these habits. Because our brain associates them with pleasure, it refuses to make us stop.

From Consciousness to Automatism: The Path of a Habit

Finally, it's interesting to note the path an action takes to become a habit. Initially, any new action requires conscious concentration. This is the "novice" phase, when we have to think every step of the way.

However, as we repeat the action, it begins to shift from our prefrontal cortex - the area of the brain responsible for conscious, complex thought - to areas of the brain associated with automation, such as the caudate nucleus and putamen. This shift frees up the prefrontal cortex to focus on other tasks, which is one reason why we can perform habits while thinking about other things.

But this process also has a counterpart. As actions become more automated, they also become more difficult to change. That's why it's often easier to implement a new habit than to change an old one. This is an important aspect to bear in mind when forming new habits or modifying old ones.

Understanding the psychology of habits is the first step in taking control of your habits. It gives you the tools to understand how habits are formed, how to change them, and how to build new, more beneficial ones. So, ready to dance to the rhythm of your neurons and sculpt

THE SEVEN PILLARS OF SUCCESS: MAKING AN INFORMED CHOICE

You may be wondering why this book focuses on seven particular habits. Why not five, ten or even a hundred? Why these seven habits and not others?

First, let me clarify where these habits come from. For many years, as an entrepreneur and habit psychology enthusiast, I've had the privilege of observing, reading, studying and interacting with many individuals who have achieved remarkable levels of success in various fields. Whether in business, sports, science, art, or even more personal areas such as health, happiness and life satisfaction, I've sought to understand what sets these successful individuals apart.

In my exploration, I discovered that despite their obvious differences in occupations, skills and circumstances, these people all shared a number of common characteristics. Digging a little deeper, I realized that these traits were not simply innate personality traits or specific talents. Rather, they were the product of deep-rooted habits, cultivated and nurtured day after day.

So, the seven habits I'm going to share with you in this book are not the result of abstract theoretical thinking. On the contrary, they are the result of careful observation and analysis of what really works in real life. These are the habits that, over and over again, have proven their effectiveness in generating success.

So why seven habits? The choice of the number seven is not arbitrary. Seven is a number that, across cultures and eras, has often been associated with the idea of fullness and completeness. But, more than the number itself, it's the variety and complementarity of these habits that are crucial. Together, these seven habits cover a wide range of aspects of our lives, from our actions to our thoughts, from our relationship with ourselves to our interaction with others.

These seven habits are not magic recipes for success. Their effectiveness lies not in their mechanical application, but in their deep integration into our way of being. They require us to engage in a process of personal transformation, in which we develop not only new routines, but also new ways of thinking, new attitudes and new perspectives.

Over the next few chapters, we'll explore these seven habits together. My hope is that this journey will provide you with valuable tools to forge your own path to success, however you personally define that term. As you discover and integrate these habits into your life, you'll be able to trigger a virtuous circle where each habit reinforces the others, creating an increasingly powerful dynamic of success.

And above all, remember this: the aim of adopting these habits is not to turn you into an inhuman productivity machine. Rather, the goal is to help you become the best version of yourself, a version that is both more efficient and more fulfilled. A version that is able to realize its deepest aspirations, while maintaining the balance and well-being necessary to enjoy the journey to the full.

There's another reason I chose these seven habits: they're universally applicable. No matter where you are in your life, whether you're a budding entrepreneur, a long-time employee, a parent or a student, these habits can help you improve your life. They transcend cultural boundaries, generations, professions and life situations. They are essentially human, rooted in our nature and psychology.

Finally, these habits are interdependent and mutually reinforcing. They form a coherent whole, and each habit adds depth and meaning to the others. You'll find that working on one habit will have ripple effects on the others, creating an upward spiral of growth and development.

The choice of these seven habits is based on careful observation of real-life success, an understanding of human psychology and a desire to provide a set of practical, effective tools for personal development. They have been tested in the heat of action by people who have achieved exceptional levels of success. They are both practical and profoundly transformative, universally applicable and deeply personal.

So I invite you to embark on this journey of exploration with an open and curious mindset, ready to experiment, learn and grow. I invite you to make the conscious choice to integrate these habits into your life and begin creating the path to success that is uniquely yours. And now, without further ado, let's begin our journey towards discovering and adopting the seven most effective habits for a successful life.

HABIT #1 - START WITH THE END IN SIGHT

LIFE ARCHITECT: DEFINING GOALS AND VISION

As captain of our ship, we've already embraced proactivity to take control of our journey. We're at the helm, ready to steer our ship to our desired destination. But where are we going? What is our destination? In other words, what are our long-term goals and vision?

If we compare our lives to building a house, defining our goals and vision is like creating the blueprints for our future home. It's a crucial exercise, requiring thought and foresight. After all, who would want a house built without a plan? How many rooms would there be? What would the kitchen look like? Where would the front door be? Without a detailed plan, the end result would be chaotic and unpredictable.

The same applies to our lives. Without clear goals and a long-term vision, we sail blindly. We risk getting lost or wasting time on roads that don't take us where we want to go. On the other hand, with a clear vision of what we want to achieve, we can direct our efforts in a focused and effective way.

Think of your vision as your personal compass, the one that guides you through storms and calm waters, helps you stay on track and reminds you why you set out on this journey in the first place. Your goals are the steps you need to take to realize that vision. They're like the markers on your map, telling you that you're moving in the right direction.

However, it's not enough to simply define goals and a vision. They need to be meaningful and aligned with our core values and aspirations. What's more, they must be clear enough to motivate us, and flexible enough to allow us to adapt our course if necessary.

How can we do this? How do we become the architect of our lives and create solid plans for our future home, our long-term vision?

The first step is to take a moment to think about what we really want in life. What do we want to achieve? What are our wildest dreams? What are our core values, and how can they guide us in our quest? These are not easy questions, but they are the most important ones we need to ask ourselves.

Once we have a clear idea of what we want, we can start defining our objectives. It's important to make them specific, measurable, achievable, relevant and time-bound, or SMART.

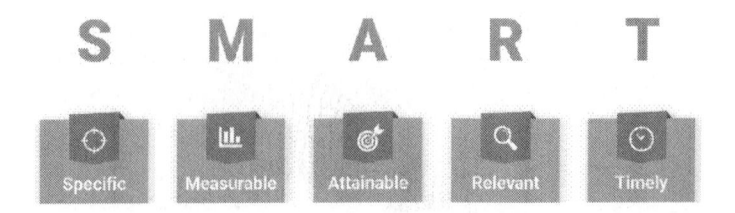

S	M	A	R	T
Specific	Measurable	Attainable	Relevant	Timely

For example, instead of saying "I want to be healthy", we could say "I want to lose 10 kilos in six months by exercising three times a week and eating healthily". This not only gives us a clear goal, but also an action plan to achieve it.

Finally, it's crucial to visualize our long-term vision. Imagine where you want to be in five, ten or even twenty years. Where are you now? Where are you now? Who's by your side? Visualize every detail of this image and feel the emotions it evokes. This vivid image will serve as your guide, inspiring and motivating you on your journey towards achieving your goals.

But being an architect doesn't just mean creating a plan and sticking to it whatever the cost. A good architect is also capable of adapting his plans to changing circumstances. Likewise, it's essential to remain flexible and open to change, while staying true to our vision. Life is unpredictable, and the paths we take to achieve our goals can change. What's important is that every step we take brings us closer to our long-term vision.

And don't be discouraged if your goals seem daunting or remote. Every great achievement begins with a small step. As Martin Luther King Jr. famously said, "You don't have to see the whole staircase, you just have to climb the first step." Trust in your ability to take those small steps toward your goals. Over time, they'll add up and you'll see how far you've come.

Becoming the architect of your life means taking control of your destiny. It's recognizing that you have the power to define your path and realize your dreams. By defining your goals and vision, you not only create a blueprint for your life, you also commit to making that blueprint a reality.

In closing, I leave you with this quote from science fiction author William Gibson: "The future is already here - it's just unevenly distributed." It's up to you to decide how you want your own future to unfold.

Remember, as the architect of your life, the vision of your future is in your hands. The pencil is in your hand, so let's start drawing.

THE POWER OF LONG-TERM VISION

The strength of long-term vision lies in its ability to provide a clear direction and purpose for all our actions. When we define a vision for our lives, we're not simply setting a goal for the future. We create a framework for our existence, a compass that guides our daily decisions and actions.

Long-term vision provides a sense of purpose. It gives us a reason to get up each morning, overcome difficulties and work hard to achieve our goals. When life gets tough, when we're tempted to give up or take shortcuts, our long-term vision reminds us why we're fighting. It gives us the motivation and perseverance to keep going, even when things don't go as planned.

At the same time, a long-term vision helps us to make coherent choices and stay focused. In today's world, it's easy to get distracted by the many opportunities and temptations that come our way. But when we have a clear vision of what we want to achieve, we're better equipped to evaluate these options and make decisions that bring us closer to our goals.

What's more, having a long-term vision can greatly enhance our self-esteem and self-confidence. By consciously working towards our ambitions, we affirm our ability to influence our future. This affirmation of our personal power can have a profoundly positive effect on how we see ourselves and our abilities.

Finally, a long-term vision enables us to live a life of purpose and meaning. It gives us a sense of being in tune with our deepest values, of working towards something greater than ourselves. It's a gratifying and fulfilling feeling that can greatly enhance our happiness and overall satisfaction with life.

A long-term vision can be a powerful tool for shaping our lives according to our desires and aspirations. It offers us clear direction, a sense of purpose, increased focus, improved self-esteem and a more meaningful life. However, having a vision is one thing, knowing how to put it into practice is quite another.

Vision Workshop: Design Your Future

Let's move on to the practical part of this chapter: the Vision Workshop. Having established the importance of a long-term vision and its impact on our lives, it's time to take action and start designing your future. This workshop consists of several exercises that will help you clarify your personal goals and develop a coherent vision for your life. Remember, there are no right or wrong answers here. The aim is to help you think in a deeper, more structured way about what you really want in life.

1. Identify your core values Core values are the beliefs and principles that guide our actions and decisions. They define what's important to us, what we value most in life. Take the time to reflect on your core values. What's most important to you? What are the principles you don't want to compromise? Write down your top three to five values.

2. Define your life domains To build a long-term vision, it's useful to divide your life into different domains. These areas could include: career, relationships, health, personal development, hobbies, etc. Write down the areas that are most relevant to you.

3. Create a vision for each area Now, for each life area you've identified, imagine what you'd like to achieve or experience in that area in 5, 10 or even 20 years' time. Try to be as specific and detailed as possible. What do you want to achieve? How would you like to feel? What would change in your life? Write these visions down.

4. Set goals to realize your vision Once you have a vision for each area of life, think about the concrete actions you can take to make that vision a reality. What are the big goals you can set to get you closer to your vision? What small steps can you take today? Write these goals down.

5. Review and refine your vision Now that you have a rough outline of your long-term vision, take the time to review it. Does it match your core values? Does it inspire and motivate you? If not, refine it until it resonates with who you are and what you want.

6. Visualize your vision Finally, take time every day to visualize your vision. Imagine you've already achieved your goals and are living the life you imagined. How do you feel? What do you see around you? Visualization can be a powerful tool to reinforce your commitment to your vision and help you stay motivated.

Creating a long-term vision can be a profoundly transformative process. It allows us to step back and think about what we really want in life, and gives us direction.

WHEN DREAMS BECOME REALITY

It's one thing to design your future, but quite another to see those designs come to life. To show you what can be achieved with a long-term vision and a concrete plan of action, I'm going to share with you two inspiring stories: that of an individual and that of an organization. These stories demonstrate the power of a long-term vision, as well as the cumulative effect of small daily actions.

Let's start with the story of an individual you probably all know: Elon Musk. Today, Musk is recognized as one of the most influential and innovative entrepreneurs of our time. Yet his success is not the result of chance or luck. Musk is the product of his own long-term vision.

From an early age, Musk had a clear vision of what he wanted to achieve: to contribute to the future of humanity by making multi-planetary living possible and accelerating the transition to sustainable energy. This vision was no mere aspiration or daydream. It was a goal he pursued with determination and perseverance, despite the many obstacles and challenges he encountered along the way.

Take SpaceX, for example. Musk founded the company in 2002 with the ambition of making space accessible to mankind. It was a bold, long-term vision, but Musk didn't stop there. He set clear, measurable goals to achieve this vision, such as sending a private rocket into orbit and developing reusable rockets. And although he encountered many setbacks and failures along the way, Musk never lost sight of his long-term vision. Today, SpaceX is at the forefront of space exploration and on the verge of realizing Musk's ambition to make space accessible to humanity.

Let's turn now to the story of an organization: Patagonia, an outdoor clothing company. Patagonia was founded on a long-term vision of "building the best product, causing no unnecessary harm, and using the company to inspire and implement solutions to the environmental crisis".

Since its inception, Patagonia has consistently worked to realize this vision through a series of sustainable and responsible initiatives. For example, the company launched the "1% for the Planet" initiative, pledging to donate 1% of its total sales to environmental organizations. It has also taken steps to reduce its carbon footprint, such as using recycled materials in its products and optimizing its operations to reduce greenhouse gas emissions.

These two stories show the power of a long-term vision. They illustrate how a clear, coherent vision can guide your actions and decisions, help you overcome challenges and lead you to success. And they also demonstrate the importance of implementing concrete actions aligned with that vision.

In Elon Musk's case, his long-term vision of making space accessible to mankind wasn't just an abstract idea. He put concrete actions in place and worked tirelessly to achieve this goal, whether developing reusable rocket technology or launching manned space missions. Musk illustrates how one individual, driven by vision and tireless determination, can achieve seemingly impossible feats.

In the case of Patagonia, the company's vision of promoting environmental sustainability is reflected not only in the products it manufactures, but also in the way it operates. Patagonia didn't wait for environmental standards to be imposed by law. Instead, it has taken a proactive approach, integrating sustainability into every aspect of its business, from supply chain to philanthropy.

These stories underline the importance of perseverance and resilience in achieving a long-term vision. Both Musk and Patagonia faced considerable challenges along the way, but they stayed true to their vision and kept moving forward, step by step.

They also demonstrate that realizing a long-term vision is not a solitary journey. It requires a team, a community, even an entire company to realize a vision. Musk didn't build SpaceX alone. He needs engineers, scientists, investors and public support to realize his vision.

Patagonia also relies on its customers, employees and partners to help promote its environmental vision.

These examples can serve as inspiration for us all. They show that, no matter how big or bold your vision, it can become reality if you're prepared to follow it with determination, set clear goals and work hard to achieve them.

So, as we continue to explore the importance of starting with the end in sight, let's keep in mind these stories of individuals and organizations who have made their dreams a reality.

HABIT #2 - MANAGING YOUR TIME - PUTTING PRIORITIES FIRST

Urgent vs Important : The Efficiency Compass

Welcome to the crossroads where the concept of urgency and importance dictate the course of our lives. By becoming aware of the distinction between these two concepts, we can better understand how our daily actions shape our reality and contribute to our personal effectiveness.

Understanding the difference between urgent and important tasks is an essential first step. Urgent tasks require immediate action. They present themselves as crises, pressing problems or looming deadlines. Sometimes these situations are truly crucial. Sometimes they seem so because they're right in front of us, demanding our attention here and now.

On the other hand, important tasks are those that contribute to our long-term goals and life mission. These tasks may not require immediate action, but they have significant value and a lasting impact on our lives. This is where activities such as personal development, strategic planning, building meaningful relationships, and maintaining our physical and mental health come in.

In the hustle and bustle of everyday life, it's easy to confuse urgency with importance. Often, we spend our days reacting to apparent emergencies, while putting aside the important tasks that, while unobtrusive, are essential to achieving our long-term vision. We then find ourselves running out of time, exhausting ourselves putting out fires instead of investing in fire prevention.

This affects our productivity in several ways. Firstly, we often waste our energy and time on tasks that seem urgent but, in reality, don't contribute significantly to our long-term goals. What's more, by focusing on the urgent, we often neglect important tasks that may not require our immediate attention, but are essential to our long-term growth and success. Finally, by constantly responding to emergencies, we can feel stressed, overwhelmed and dissatisfied, as our lives seem to be dictated by external circumstances rather than our conscious choices.

The trick to navigating this dilemma is to learn to differentiate between the urgent and the important, and to act accordingly. U.S. President Dwight D. Eisenhower illustrated this concept well with what is now known as the "Eisenhower Matrix". According to this principle, we should divide our tasks into four categories: Urgent and Important, Not Urgent but Important, Urgent but Not Important, and Not Urgent and Not Important. The idea is to minimize the time spent on unimportant tasks, whether urgent or not, and increase the time spent on important tasks, especially those that are not urgent.

	URGENT	NOT URGENT
IMPORTANT	<u>Quadrant I</u> *urgent and important* **DO**	<u>Quadrant II</u> *not urgent but important* **PLAN**
NOT IMPORTANT	<u>Quadrant III</u> *urgent but not important* **DELEGATE**	<u>Quadrant IV</u> *not urgent and not important* **ELIMINATE**

By becoming masters of this distinction and applying it to our daily lives, we can reverse the pattern of reactive restlessness and embark on a path of proactive action, aligned with our real priorities.

Take personal development, for example. It can be easy to put off learning a new skill or reading an informative book, because these activities may seem less urgent than answering e-mails or completing a report for work. However, in the long term, these activities contribute to your growth and your ability to achieve your life goals. Ignoring important but non-urgent tasks is like ignoring the gyroscope guiding your ship - you risk finding yourself off course, or worse, adrift.

Likewise, consider your health. It's easy to neglect healthy eating or regular exercise in the midst of the urgent demands of daily life. But in the long run, these decisions can have devastating consequences on your health and well-being and could even turn into urgent crises if left untreated.

It's also important to recognize that not everything that's urgent is necessarily important. The constant demands on our attention - the notifications on our phone, the e-mails that demand an immediate response, the routine tasks that always seem urgent - often don't contribute significantly to our long-term goals. In fact, they can distract us from achieving our goals.

The key to efficiency lies in our ability to distinguish the urgent from the important, and to prioritize what is truly essential to us. This may mean rethinking the way we organize our time and activities. It may mean saying no to certain urgent demands to make room for what's really important. And it may require taking a long-term perspective, looking beyond the hustle and bustle of the present moment to focus on what will really help us achieve our long-term ambitions.

Ultimately, understanding the difference between urgent and important tasks is more than just a time management strategy. It's a philosophy of life that invites us to think deeply about what really matters to us, and to make conscious choices to honor those priorities in our daily lives. By adopting this approach, we can not only improve our efficiency, but also find greater satisfaction and meaning in our work and our lives.

THE MAGIC OF 80/20: THE SECRET OF PRIORITIES

The 80/20 principle, also known as Pareto's Law, is a powerful concept that can radically transform your approach to priorities. It's named after Vilfredo Pareto, a 19th-century Italian economist, who observed that 80% of the land in Italy was owned by 20% of the population. He also observed that this ratio was reproduced in various other areas of life and society.

To put the 80/20 principle into a personal context, consider this: 80% of your success could come from 20% of your efforts. It's a powerful idea, but what does it mean in practice?

It's important to note that the 80/20 figures are not absolute; rather, they represent a general trend. It's not necessarily the exact division in every case, but it's an observation that frequently holds true. The idea is that the majority of your results come from a small portion of your efforts.

For example, you may discover that 20% of your daily tasks contribute to 80% of your overall productivity. Or that 20% of your customers generate 80% of your income. Or that 20% of your health habits contribute to 80% of your overall well-being.

To harness the magic of 80/20, start by taking stock of ir activities, projects and tasks. Identify what brings the most value and ask yourself: "What actions generate the most positive results in my life?". These are the activities that make up your key 20%.

I too was rather dubious about this "law" at first. I found it almost impossible. So one day I decided to do the math myself on certain aspects of my life.

In one of my online sales businesses, I started to calculate how many products were making me the most money. I'll let you in on the rest ... 17.8% of my products brought in 82.3% of my sales. That's almost 20% for 80%, so you get the idea. And this applies to many other things. I'll let you work it out for yourself, you'll be amazed.

Let's get back to where we were. The next step is to think about how you can increase the time and energy you devote to these key activities. This may mean delegating, eliminating or minimizing some of the other tasks that take up your time but don't bring as much value.

It's essential to understand that not all tasks are created equal. Some efforts have a disproportionate impact on our results, and our challenge is to identify them and give them the attention they deserve.

Applying the 80/20 principle is not an exact science. It requires intuition, reflection and a willingness to experiment. However, when you start applying this rule, you can discover a new world of efficiency and productivity.

You can realize that you're capable of accomplishing more - much more - with less.

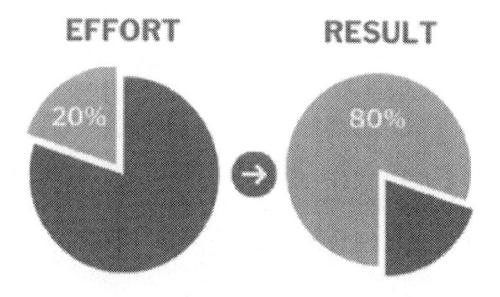

EFFORT **RESULT**

20% → 80%

By applying the 80/20 principle, you can not only improve your productivity, but also save time for what really matters to you. You can focus your energy on the tasks that bring the most value, instead of spreading yourself too thinly over a multitude of minor tasks.

And, perhaps most importantly, you may discover that the secret to efficiency lies not in doing more, but in doing better. That is, focusing on the tasks that have the greatest impact.

Let's take a concrete example to illustrate this idea. Imagine you're an entrepreneur and you spend your time between customer meetings, product development, employee management and administrative paperwork. Applying the 80/20 principle, you realize that 80% of your revenue comes from 20% of your customers (much like my previous example). So you decide to devote more time to these key customers and delegate some of your other tasks.

The result? Your business prospers more than ever, and you even have more free time.

Or, if you're a student, you may find that 80% of your success in class comes from 20% of your study habits (going to the library, rereading your lessons at night, making flashcards, that sort of thing). By focusing on these effective study methods and eliminating distractions, you can dramatically improve your grades while having more time for extracurricular activities.

The 80/20 principle is a powerful way of reviewing your priorities and identifying where your efforts will pay off most. It allows you to focus on what's really important, rather than spreading yourself too thinly over tasks that don't contribute significantly to your goals.

Ultimately, the "magic" of 80/20 is that it gives us permission to do less to achieve more. It reminds us that the key to effectiveness lies in the quality of our efforts, not the quantity. And it encourages us to be more intentional and selective in how we invest our time and energy.

Implementing the 80/20 principle in your life may seem daunting at first. But remember, it's not about changing everything at once. Start small. Identify a single task, project or habit on which you can apply this rule. Over time, you'll be able to extend your approach to other areas of your life and see a significant improvement in your efficiency and productivity.

Ultimately, the 80/20 principle is not just a time management or productivity strategy. It's a philosophy of life. An approach that encourages us to focus on what really matters, to be more aware of how we use our time, and to make choices that bring us closer to our deepest goals and visions. The 80/20 principle isn't just a formula for efficiency, it's a roadmap to a more intentional and fulfilled life.

MASTER OF TIME: THE ART OF ORGANIZATION

Take a jar, fill it with large stones until it's full, then ask the people around you if the jar is full. Most people will answer "yes". Then take some smaller stones and pour them into the jar. The pebbles slip into the empty spaces between the large stones. Let's ask again, is the jar full? Some might say "yes", others might begin to understand the principle.

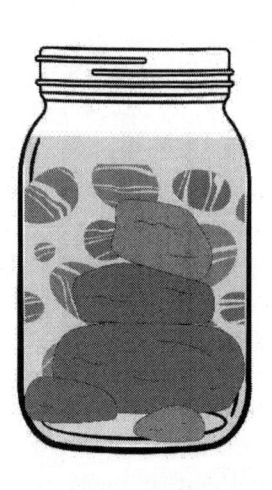

Continue the experiment by adding sand. The sand will work its way into the small remaining spaces. Is the jar full now? For everyone, the answer is "yes". Then pour water into the jar. The water seeps between the grains of sand, filling every available gap. The jar is really full now.

This experience is a powerful metaphor for the organization of our time. The big stones represent the most important tasks, the priorities that bring us closer to our goals. The pebbles represent secondary tasks which, while necessary, are not as critical as the big stones. Sand represents the routine tasks, the small details that fill our day, while water represents the unexpected distractions that tend to creep into our schedule.

If we fill our jar (our day) first with sand and water (the routine tasks and distractions), there will be no room left for the stones and pebbles (the priority and secondary tasks). On the other hand, if we start with the large stones, then add the pebbles, sand and water, everything fits perfectly into the jar.

The same applies to the organization of our time. If we start with priority tasks, we ensure that they are taken care of. Then we can deal with the secondary tasks, and finally, we take care of the routines and the unexpected. In this way, we ensure that we devote our time and energy to the things that matter most.

Becoming a master of your own time requires a clear awareness of your priorities and a willingness to structure your day around them. It means saying "no" to certain requests and delegating certain tasks. It also means learning to manage distractions and resisting the urge to do things that seem urgent but aren't really important.

There are many time organization techniques and methods you can adopt, from the Pomodoro method to the Time Blocking technique. The key is to find the method that works best for you and adapt it to your specific needs.

-

The Pomodoro method, named after the tomato-shaped kitchen timer (pomodoro in Italian) used by its creator, is a time management technique that encourages periods of concentrated work interspersed with breaks. It works quite simply: you work for a set period of time, usually 25 minutes, then take a 5-minute break. This sequence is called a "Pomodoro". After four "Pomodoros", we take a longer break, usually of 15 to 30 minutes. This rhythm keeps you focused and productive, without overloading or tiring you.

The Time Blocking technique involves dividing your day into blocks of time reserved for specific tasks. For example, you could set aside a block of time in the morning to work on an important project, another block after lunch to answer your e-mails, and so on. The idea is to focus on one task at a time, rather than getting distracted by multiple simultaneous tasks. By setting aside blocks of time for certain activities, you can ensure that you have enough time for the most important tasks. I personally use this method the most and recommend it to you.

Keep in mind that the goal of time management is not to fill every minute of your day with productive work. Balance is crucial. Time for rest, relaxation, leisure, family and friends is just as important. These moments of pause are like the water that hydrates the sands of your life, keeping them agile and preventing them from congealing into a compact, inflexible block. We're not robots, so it's impossible for anyone to work 14 hours a day on the most important tasks 365 days a year without ever taking a break.

The art of organization goes beyond the simple execution of tasks. It's a skill that involves knowing when to work, when to rest, when to commit and when to withdraw. It's a delicate balance that demands attention and discipline, but also flexibility and adaptability.

Effective time management is a journey rather than a destination. You will inevitably encounter obstacles and challenges along the way. There will be days when your plan doesn't work as planned, when unforeseen emergencies upset your schedule. When this happens, don't be discouraged. Be resilient, adjust your plan and keep moving forward.

Remember the jar in our experiment. Imagine that every morning, you wake up to an empty jar. It's up to you to decide how you want to fill it. You can fill it with sand and water, and find that the stones and pebbles don't fit, or you can start with the big stones, add the pebbles, then the sand, and finally the water. The choice is yours.

Becoming a master of your own time is no easy task, but it's a challenge worth taking on. It's an investment in your future, a skill that can transform your life. By mastering your time, you can achieve your goals, realize your dreams and live a life of success and fulfillment.

THE ANTI-PROCRASTINATION SHIELD

Procrastination. That word that weighs heavily on our shoulders and is the sworn enemy of productivity. Yet we've all succumbed to its tempting call at one time or another. But imagine for a moment being able to raise a shield against this scourge of productivity, one that would enable you to stay focused and accomplish your tasks with determination. This shield exists and is within your reach. To erect it, you need to master certain concrete time management and planning techniques.

Be the master of your routine like Tim Ferriss

One of the people best known for effective time management is Tim Ferriss, author of the bestseller "The 4-Hour Week". Ferriss is famous for his optimal use of time and his innovative techniques for increasing productivity.

For Ferriss, the art of overcoming procrastination lies in setting up routines and automating tasks. He uses what he calls "time rules" to structure his day. These rules include eliminating non-essential tasks, outsourcing tasks that don't require his specific expertise, and focusing his energy on what produces the most important results.

Embracing monotony like Jerry Seinfeld

Comedian Jerry Seinfeld has a simple but effective technique for countering procrastination, known as "not breaking the chain". The technique involves accomplishing a specific task each day, then marking that day on a calendar. The aim is to create an unbroken chain of marks on the calendar, stimulating motivation to keep working each day so as not to "break the chain".

Focus on the essentials like Warren Buffet

Warren Buffet, one of the world's most successful investors, has a unique approach to time management. He concentrates on one task at a time. This is Buffet's "top 5" strategy. He writes a list of 25 goals, selects five as absolute priorities and completely ignores the other 20 until the top five are achieved.

Dedicate yourself to periods of intense concentration like Cal Newport

Cal Newport, author of "Deep Work", encourages periods of intense, uninterrupted concentration. Newport suggests devoting long periods of time to carrying out tasks requiring deep concentration, without distractions. He claims that this practice enables high-quality work to be accomplished in less time.

Stay motivated like Elon Musk

Sometimes, the best way to overcome procrastination is to find a source of motivation. Take Elon Musk, for example. He's famous for his ability to juggle several ambitious projects simultaneously. Musk, CEO of SpaceX and Tesla, attributes his success to an extremely disciplined work routine and intense motivation. He works an average of 80-90 hours a week, focusing on the essentials and avoiding distractions. He finds his motivation in solving the most challenging problems of our time, such as interplanetary travel and renewable energies.

Fighting the fear of starting like Mark Twain

Mark Twain once said: "If it's your job to swallow one frog, it's better to do it in the morning, and if it's your job to swallow two frogs, it's better to swallow the bigger one first". This quote is often used to illustrate the concept of "eating the toad", i.e. doing the most difficult task first every day. Fear of starting a difficult task can often drive us to procrastinate. By doing this task first, we eliminate this fear and increase our productivity for the rest of the day.

Create a productivity habit like Stephen King

Writer Stephen King has a rigorous daily routine to maintain his productivity. He commits to writing 2,000 words a day, whatever the circumstances. By creating this habit, he has managed to write more than 50 novels over the course of his career. It's not just about working hard, but working regularly, creating a habit of productivity.

The key to building an effective anti-procrastination shield lies in adopting concrete time management and planning techniques, backed by strong motivation and unshakeable determination. By taking control of your time and establishing routines, you can maximize your efficiency and avoid the pitfalls of procrastination. Remember: time is your most precious resource. So it's essential to learn how to manage it carefully.

HABIT #3 - BE PROACTIVE

Captaining your Ship: The Nature of Proactivity

When we talk about proactivity, we're talking about a true internal compass that guides us through the ocean of life. We become the captain of our own ship, making decisions and taking actions that shape our course, rather than simply being pushed along by the waves of circumstance. So, what is proactivity? And why is it so crucial to steering our lives?

Proactivity is a mindset that encourages us to act rather than react. Proactive people take the initiative, plan ahead and anticipate problems before they arise. They are not simply passive in the face of their environment, but take action to influence their surroundings and their future. They don't see the world as something that happens to them, but as something they can help shape.

On the contrary, reactivity is a posture of reacting to events after they've happened, often emotionally or impulsively. Reactive people are often passive, allowing their environment to determine their actions and their future.

The difference between these two attitudes can be illustrated with a maritime metaphor. Imagine you're sailing on the high seas. If you're reactive, you wait for the winds and currents to push you along, and adapt to their direction. You can end up being swept away where you don't want to go, or even run aground on reefs.

On the other hand, if you're proactive, you set your course and adjust your sails to reach your destination, whatever the weather conditions. You're ready to face storms and sail through them to stay on course.

This distinction is essential in all areas of life, whether it's our career, our relationships, our health or our personal development. Proactivity is the driving force that enables us to define our goals, take action to achieve them and overcome the obstacles that stand in our way.

In the workplace, for example, proactive people don't just wait for instructions. They actively seek ways to improve their performance, increase productivity and contribute to the achievement of corporate objectives. They anticipate problems and propose solutions before they become critical.

In relationships, proactive people take the initiative to resolve conflicts, communicate openly and build strong relationships. They don't wait for problems to escalate or for the other person to make the first move.

When it comes to health, proactive people take care of their bodies by exercising regularly, eating healthily and avoiding harmful behaviors. They don't just wait for illness to strike before starting to take care of themselves.

In the field of personal development, proactivity means a constant commitment to learning, growing and improving. Proactive people don't wait for opportunities to come to them, they actively seek them out. They are always on the lookout for new skills to acquire, new knowledge to learn, and new experiences to live.

However, it's important to note that proactivity isn't simply a matter of "doing more". It's not about overloading yourself with work or pushing yourself beyond your limits. Being proactive also means knowing when to step back, rest and recharge. It's understanding that we can't control every situation and event in our lives, but we can always control our attitude and reactions.

Being the captain of your own ship also means knowing when to sail at full speed, when to slow down, and when to simply let the ship rest. Proactivity is a question of balancing action and reflection, effort and relaxation, control and letting go.

Ultimately, proactivity is the catalyst that enables us to turn our dreams into reality. It gives us the power to define our destiny and create the life we want to live. Without proactivity, we're at the mercy of life's winds and currents. With proactivity, we become the masters of our destiny, able to sail confidently towards our goals, whatever challenges life may throw at us.

But being proactive isn't always easy. It requires courage, determination and a constant willingness to learn and improve.

FORGING YOUR PROACTIVITY

Now that we have a clear understanding of what proactivity is, it's time to look at how we can cultivate it in our lives. As we saw earlier, being proactive isn't just about "doing more". It's about taking deliberate decisions and actions to create the life we want. In this section, we'll explore tips and strategies for developing a proactive mindset.

1. Develop a clear vision

The first step in becoming proactive is to develop a clear vision of what you want to achieve. This is your internal compass, the guide that will help you navigate through life's challenges and opportunities. To develop your vision, take a moment to think about what's really important to you, what you want to achieve in your life, and what you want to become. This vision will help you stay motivated and focused, even when the going gets tough. It's all about finding your "why". Why do you want to improve in this particular area of your life? This will help you stay on track.

2. Plan your trip

Once you have a clear vision, it's time to start planning your trip. Proactivity doesn't mean acting impulsively or without thought. On the contrary, it means taking the time to reflect on your actions and carefully plan your path to success. What steps do you need to take to realize your vision? What obstacles might you encounter along the way, and how can you overcome them? With a clear plan in mind, you'll be better equipped to take proactive action.

3. Take concrete action

Proactivity is useless without action. Once you have a vision and a plan, it's time to take action. Don't just wait for opportunities to come your way. Actively seek them out. Whether it's acquiring a new skill, applying for a promotion, or starting a new project, be ready to take the first step. Every action you take brings you closer to your vision.

4. Cultivate resilience

Being proactive doesn't mean that everything will always go according to plan. There will be challenges and setbacks along the way. That's why it's important to cultivate resilience. Resilience is the ability to pick yourself up after failure, learn from your mistakes, and keep moving forward, even when the going gets tough. By developing your resilience, you'll be better equipped to face challenges and remain proactive, even in difficult situations.

These strategies are a starting point for developing a proactive mindset. By applying them in your life, you'll begin to take control of your destiny and actively navigate towards your goals.

FROM IDEA TO ACTION: THE STORY OF EFFICIENCY

It's said that a picture is worth a thousand words. When it comes to understanding proactivity, perhaps a story is worth even more. Let me tell you Sarah's story.

Sarah was a young woman who had always had a passion for fashion. From an early age, she had dreamed of creating her own line of clothing, but she had always thought that this was just an unattainable dream. After all, she had no experience in the fashion industry, and she didn't know anyone who could help her get started. So she settled into a comfortable but unsatisfying office job, and put her dream on the back burner.

However, something changed in Sarah when she read a book on proactivity. She realized that if she wanted her dream to come true, she would have to take the initiative to make it happen. Instead of waiting for an opportunity, she decided to create it.

Sarah began by defining a clear vision of what she wanted to achieve: a clothing line that combined comfort and style, that was both elegant and casual. Then she drew up a plan. She spent hours researching the fashion industry, learning how garment production worked, and understanding the design process. She took sewing and design classes, and spent evenings and weekends creating samples of her designs.

It hasn't been an easy road. Sarah has encountered many obstacles, from finding fabric suppliers to struggling to finance her business. But each time, she found a way to overcome these challenges. She used her proactivity to find solutions, like forging partnerships with other fashion entrepreneurs to share production costs, or launching a crowdfunding campaign to finance her first collection.

Eventually, Sarah's hard work paid off. Her first collection was a success, and her clothing line began to make a name for itself in the fashion industry. She had turned her dream into reality, not by waiting for opportunities to present themselves, but by taking the initiative to create them.

Sarah's story is a powerful example of proactivity in action. It shows us that, no matter the size of our dream or the scale of the challenges we face, we have the power to take action to make that dream a reality. We are not passive passengers in our lives, but captains of our own ship.

Sarah isn't a superhero. She's an ordinary person, just like you and me. What sets her apart is her proactive mentality. She's decided not to wait for things to happen, but to make them happen. And if Sarah can do that, so can we.

So, what can we learn from Sarah's story? Three essential points.

- First, Sarah took control of her situation. She wasn't happy with her current work situation and had a dream she was passionate about. Instead of settling for what she had and waiting for an opportunity to present itself, she decided to take action to change her situation. She was the captain of her ship, deciding which direction to take.

- Secondly, Sarah acted with determination. Once she decided to pursue her dream, she didn't just half-ass it. She dove headlong into her project, learning everything she could about the fashion industry and working hard to create her designs. She was proactive, not only in making the decision to pursue her dream, but also in doing whatever it took to make it a reality.

- Finally, Sarah showed resilience. She encountered many obstacles along the way, but she never gave up. Every time she encountered an obstacle, she found a way to overcome it. She used her proactivity to find solutions to her problems, instead of letting them discourage her.

Sarah's story is a powerful illustration of what proactivity is all about. It's not just about making decisions, but also about action, determination and resilience. It's a mindset that enables us to take control of our lives and steer them in the direction we want.

Remember: you too can be like Sarah. You too can be the captain of your own ship. You too can take action to make your dreams come true. Proactivity is within everyone's grasp; all it takes is the courage to seize it. So what are you waiting for? It's time to take the reins of your life and become the master of your destiny.

SURVIVAL KIT FOR THE PROACTIVE

When you feel overwhelmed by life's challenges, remember that you are the captain of your ship. Remember that you have the power to choose how you will react to situations, and that every choice you make brings you a little closer to your desired destination.

Take a moment to reflect on the techniques you've learned. How can you integrate them into your daily life? Perhaps you could start by making a clear plan for the day or week ahead. By defining precise objectives, you give direction to your proactivity. Then, build periods of reflection into your routine to assess your progress and readjust your course if necessary.

Then think about the people you admire for their proactivity. How do they turn their ideas into action? Perhaps you could adopt some of their strategies or, better still, adapt them to suit your own needs and circumstances. You could also look for inspiration in the stories of people who have successfully overcome obstacles thanks to their proactivity. These anecdotes can provide you with concrete examples of how proactivity can transform your life.

And don't forget that proactivity is a muscle you can develop. The more you exercise it, the stronger it becomes.

So don't be afraid to start small. Every step, no matter how small, brings you a little closer to your goal.

Finally, remember that proactivity is not just a skill to be developed, but a way of life. It's not just about doing, but about being. By cultivating a proactive mindset, you're not only sailing towards your goals, you're also creating a richer, more satisfying life.

Therein lies your proactivity survival kit. It's simple, but powerful. It contains no magic wand or miracle potion. It's made up of proven tools, inspiring ideas and fundamental principles. But most importantly, it contains something only you can provide: your commitment to being the captain of your ship, taking control of your life and making your vision a reality.

HABIT #4 - SEEK TO UNDERSTAND, THEN TO BE UNDERSTOOD

THE GIFT OF LISTENING: THE IMPORTANCE OF ACTIVE LISTENING

In the hustle and bustle of our daily lives, between tasks to be accomplished, problems to be solved and goals to be achieved, we often forget a fundamental, yet natural human skill: observation. But not just any observation, the kind I call intentional observation.

Too often, we forget that every detail, every element of our environment, every gesture or facial expression of our interlocutor can be a precious source of information. We tend to see without really looking, to hear without really listening. This habit leads us to miss out on valuable information that could help us better understand our environment and the people with whom we interact.

Intentional observation goes far beyond distracted looking or passive listening. It involves conscious presence and active attention to our surroundings. It's about really looking, really listening, really perceiving our environment in all its richness and complexity.

But why is this so important? Because better observation leads to better understanding. When we take the time to observe carefully, we begin to see details we might otherwise have missed. We begin to understand the subtle nuances of non-verbal communication. We begin to see the hidden motivations behind others' actions. We begin to understand the complex dynamics at work in our environment.

Take the example of a business leader who wants to improve his team's productivity. Rather than rushing to implement new strategies or processes, he could start by simply observing. By taking the time to carefully observe his team at work, he might begin to see problems or inefficiencies he'd never thought of before. Perhaps some team members are overworked, while others are under-utilized. Maybe some processes are redundant or unnecessary. Maybe some meetings are too long or inefficient. These are just hypotheses, but they could never be identified without careful observation.

Similarly, in our personal relationships, intentional observation can be a valuable source of information. By carefully observing our partner's behavior, we can begin to understand what motivates them, what worries them, what makes them happy. We can see the subtle signs of stress or discomfort before they become real problems. We can better understand their needs and desires, and thus better meet their expectations.

Amplificateur de Communication : Ameliorer ses Competences

Following on logically from intentional observation, introspective reflection is the next step towards better understanding, and thus better action. If intentional observation enables us to gather valuable information about our environment and others, introspective reflection enables us to integrate and use it to improve our self-knowledge.

Introspective reflection is the art of asking ourselves the right questions, confronting our own thoughts and feelings, taking stock of our motivations and desires, our strengths and weaknesses. It's about taking the time to pause, to detach ourselves from the hustle and bustle of daily life and turn inwards, towards our own consciousness.

It's a practice that requires honesty and courage, as it involves facing truths that may be uncomfortable or disturbing. But it's also an extremely gratifying practice, as it enables us to understand ourselves better, make more informed decisions and live a more authentic and fulfilling life.

Here are some tips and tricks to help you practice introspective reflection effectively:

1. **Take time**: Introspective reflection isn't something you can do in a hurry. It takes time to detach ourselves from our daily concerns, to turn inward and explore our thoughts and feelings. Take

the time to make yourself comfortable, breathe deeply and focus on your mind.

2. **Be open and honest**: Introspective reflection requires honesty. There's no point in lying to yourself or avoiding certain thoughts or feelings because they're uncomfortable or disturbing. Be open to whatever arises, welcoming it with kindness and honesty.

3. **Use a journal**: Writing is an excellent tool for introspective reflection. It allows you to express your thoughts and feelings in a more structured way, to examine them in greater detail and to store them for future reflection. Try to write regularly in a journal, even if it's just a few lines a day.

4. **Ask yourself the right questions**: Introspective thinking isn't just passive introspection, it's an active investigation of yourself. Ask yourself questions like: What do I really feel? Why do I react the way I do? What does this say about me? What would I really like? What are my strengths? What are my weaknesses?

5. **Be patient and kind to yourself**: Introspective reflection can be a difficult and sometimes painful process. Be patient with yourself, don't judge or criticize yourself. Be kind to yourself, welcoming your thoughts and feelings with love and understanding.

6. **Make room for silence**: In our noisy, hectic modern society, silence has become a rare commodity. Yet it is in silence that we can truly hear ourselves. Make room for silence in your life, even if it's only a few minutes a day. It's in these moments of silence that the deepest truths can emerge.

7. **Practice meditation**: Meditation is an age-old practice that can greatly facilitate introspective reflection. By helping us to calm our minds and focus our attention, meditation creates a space conducive to introspection. There are many forms of meditation, from simple attention to the breath to more complex techniques. Choose the one that suits you best.

These introspective reflection techniques are not miracle solutions. They take time, effort and patience. But the benefits are worth it. By taking the time to understand ourselves, we acquire a deep self-knowledge that is both a valuable guide for our lives and a source of strength and confidence.

Introspective reflection is like a journey into our own minds. It's not always an easy journey, and it can sometimes take us to dark or unfamiliar places. But it's also an exciting and enriching journey, one that allows us to discover our true selves, our passions, our dreams, our fears and our hopes.

So, by improving our self-knowledge through introspective reflection, we can become more authentic, empathetic and effective interlocutors. We can communicate with greater clarity and conviction, understand others with greater depth and nuance, and act with greater confidence and determination. In short, we can become the authors of our own story, rather than mere spectators.

So, I invite you to embark on this journey of introspection, to ask yourself those tough questions, to face those uncomfortable truths, to explore those uncharted territories of your mind. I promise you'll emerge transformed, more aware, more authentic and more fulfilled. And it's through this personal transformation that you'll be able to truly influence the world around you.

THE POWER OF UNDERSTANDING: INSPIRING ANECDOTES

I'd like to share an anecdote from my life that perfectly illustrates the power of understanding. It was when I was just beginning my career as a business coach. I had been hired by a well-established technology company, with the aim of resolving an internal conflict that was threatening the team's productivity.

On my first day, I met Robert, a senior developer respected for his technical genius, but known to be difficult to deal with. Other team members were complaining about his dismissive attitude and lack of interest in their ideas.

Robert, for his part, was frustrated by what he perceived as his colleagues' lack of competence.

My first reaction was to talk to Robert and advise him to be more respectful towards his colleagues. He reacted defensively, saying he was there to do his job, not to make friends. It was obvious that my approach wasn't working.

So I decided to change tactics. Instead of trying to tell him what to do, I tried to understand his point of view. I spent time with him, observing how he worked and listening to what he had to say.

To my surprise, I discovered that Robert was extremely passionate about his work and frustrated because he couldn't communicate his ideas effectively. He wasn't dismissive of others; he just didn't know how to engage with them productively.

With this new understanding, I was able to help Robert improve his communication skills. We worked together to find ways for him to share his ideas more constructively and to be open to suggestions from his colleagues.

Over time, the atmosphere in the team began to change. The other members began to appreciate Robert's passion and commitment to quality work. Robert, for his part, learned to value his colleagues' contributions and see them as allies rather than obstacles.

This experience left a deep impression on me and taught me a valuable lesson. The true power of understanding lies not only in the ability to resolve conflicts or overcome misunderstandings. It lies in the ability to create connections, build bridges, transform relationships.

It's a powerful tool for bringing about positive change, and a habit we should all seek to cultivate.

HABIT #5 - THINK WIN-WIN

BEYOND COMPETITION: THE HARMONY OF COOPERATION

In a world where the emphasis is often on competition and individualism, the idea of collaboration and cooperation may seem counter-intuitive. Yet it's an essential habit for those who aspire to personal and professional fulfillment. To understand this, let's take a detour into the world of sport.

Soccer is a sport where the spirit of competition is particularly strong. Every team wants to win, and every player wants to shine. But what distinguishes a good team from a great one is its ability to collaborate and cooperate. Lionel Messi, one of the greatest footballers of all time, is famous not only for his ability to score goals, but also for his ability to cooperate with his team-mates, to pass the ball when necessary and to support the team as a whole. His success is the fruit of collaboration.

In business, this notion is just as relevant. Steve Jobs, the iconic founder of Apple, succeeded in revolutionizing many industries by encouraging cooperation and collaboration within his teams. Jobs had a clear vision of what he wanted to achieve, but he also knew he couldn't do it alone. So he recruited talented people and encouraged them to work together, share ideas and solve problems together. Apple's spectacular success is testimony to the power of this approach.

Cooperative harmony is based on the idea that, in many cases, "one plus one can equal three". When two or more people work together, they can achieve things they couldn't on their own. This synergy, which lies at the heart of cooperation, makes it possible to achieve results that are greater than the sum of individual efforts.

That said, cooperation is not just a question of efficiency. It's also a question of ethics. By collaborating with others, by sharing our resources and skills, we recognize that we are all interconnected, that the success of one does not necessarily come at the expense of others. This recognition of interdependence is essential to building a fairer, more caring society.

To implement this habit, it's important to adopt a collaborative mindset, actively seeking ways to cooperate with others, even in situations where competition seems to be the norm. This involves developing skills such as active listening, negotiation, problem-solving and teamwork.

But above all, it requires a change of perspective. Instead of seeing others as adversaries, we must learn to see them as partners, allies. We need to remember that, while we may pursue our own goals, we all share the same fundamental desire: to be happy, to succeed and to contribute to something greater than ourselves.

In doing so, we don't just change the way we see the world; we change the world itself. As the American anthropologist Margaret Mead so aptly put it: "Never doubt that a small group of thoughtful, committed citizens can change the world. In fact, that's always how the world has changed."

One of the simplest ways to foster cooperation is to create opportunities for collaboration. In a professional context, this can take the form of team projects, brainstorming sessions or group training courses. In a personal context, it could mean joining a club, getting involved in a cause you care about, or simply spending quality time with loved ones.

Cooperation doesn't necessarily mean agreeing on everything. In fact, a diversity of perspectives can be a valuable asset. The important thing is to respect the opinions of others, be open to discussion and seek solutions that meet the needs of all participants.

However, cooperation must not be forced. To be genuine, it must stem from a sincere desire to help others and contribute to a common goal. Only by being genuinely committed to cooperation can we truly reap its rewards.

Finally, it's crucial to celebrate our collective successes. By recognizing each other's contributions and celebrating what we've achieved together, we strengthen the bonds that bind us and encourage a culture of cooperation.

Cooperation is more than just a strategy for achieving our goals. It's a philosophy of life, an approach that recognizes that we're all in this together, and that we have much to gain by working together. By cultivating the harmony of cooperation, we can not only enrich our lives, but also contribute to a more united and equitable world.

CREATING VALUE: BUILDING MUTUALLY BENEFICIAL RELATIONSHIPS

Being a value creator means not only doing what's necessary to achieve your own goals, but also helping others to achieve theirs. It's the art of establishing mutually beneficial relationships that are both satisfying and productive for all parties involved.

A mutually beneficial relationship is like a dance. It requires perfect synchronization, understanding and appreciation of the other. It's a symbiosis where each partner draws on the strengths of the other, creates harmony and progresses together towards a common goal.

Building such relationships begins with a deep understanding of yourself and others. Understanding what motivates you, what excites you, what drives you, is the first step to understanding how you can bring value to others. At the same time, understanding the needs, desires and aspirations of others is the key to understanding how they can bring value to you.

Take a business partnership, for example. Two entrepreneurs might have complementary skills - one might be good at sales, while the other might have technical expertise in marketing. Together, they can create a business that is greater than the sum of its parts.

Similarly, in a friendly or loving relationship, both partners can bring unique qualities to the relationship that enrich the other's life. One partner can be a great listener, while the other can be an enthusiastic motivator. Together, they can create a dynamic that supports and uplifts both.

But how do you create such a dynamic? There are several key principles that can help build mutually beneficial relationships.

- The first principle is mutual respect. Each person has their own intrinsic value and deserves to be treated with dignity and respect. Mutual respect creates a safe environment where individuals feel valued and appreciated for who they are and what they bring to the relationship.

- The second principle is open communication. Honest and transparent communication is essential to understanding the needs and expectations of others. It also enables misunderstandings and conflicts to be resolved constructively.

- The third principle is mutual contribution. Each party must contribute to the relationship in a way that is meaningful to them. This creates a sense of fairness and balance, where each person feels valued for their contribution.

- The fourth principle is mutual growth and development. Mutually beneficial relationships are dynamic and evolving. They offer opportunities to learn, grow and develop, both individually and together.

Being a creator of value means going beyond the simple "me" to embrace the "we". It means recognizing that we are all interconnected, that our actions have consequences for others, and that we all have something valuable to bring to the table. By cultivating mutually beneficial relationships,

PACIFIC NEGOTIATOR: CONFLICT RESOLUTION STRATEGIES

The peaceful negotiator: this term seems almost contradictory at first glance. After all, negotiations and conflicts are often perceived as environments fraught with adversity, confrontation and rivalry. However, it's crucial to recognize that an effective negotiator is not one who walks out of the conference room with the spoils, leaving behind a ruined battlefield. On the contrary, a peaceful negotiator is one who succeeds in forging mutually beneficial and lasting agreements, transforming differences into opportunities for fruitful cooperation.

So how do you become a peaceful negotiator? Here are some strategies that can help you successfully navigate the complex maze of conflict resolution.

Strategy 1: Preparation

Every successful negotiation begins with careful preparation. Know your objectives, needs and limitations, as well as those of the other party. A thorough understanding of what's at stake and what motivates each party makes for a more balanced and enlightened negotiation.

Strategy 2: Active listening

Active listening is an essential skill for any peaceful negotiator. It involves paying full attention to the other party, understanding their point of view and showing empathy. By showing that you respect and value their ideas, you establish a climate of trust and mutual respect.

Strategy 3: Clear and Respectful Communication

Communication is the most powerful tool in any negotiation. Be clear and precise about what you want, but avoid being aggressive or condescending. Respectful communication helps to ease tensions and promote constructive dialogue.

Strategy 4: Seek win-win solutions

Instead of fighting for the biggest piece of the cake, look for ways to make the cake bigger for everyone. Look for solutions that satisfy the needs of all parties. This may require creativity and flexibility, but the result will be a lasting agreement that benefits everyone.

Strategy 5: Managing emotions

Negotiations can be emotionally charged. A peaceful negotiator knows how to manage his or her own emotions and those of others. Remain calm, even in the face of adversity, and use empathy to understand and soothe the other party's negative emotions.

Strategy 6: Remain Patient and Persevering

Conflict resolution is often a long and complex process. It's important to remain patient and not rush to reach an agreement at any cost. Sometimes it takes time to find the right solution.

Becoming a peaceful negotiator is no easy task. It requires skill, practice and a certain amount of courage. However, the rewards are considerable. As a peaceful negotiator, you have the power to turn conflict into opportunity, to build bridges instead of walls, and to forge lasting relationships based on mutual respect and cooperation. You become not only an agent of positive change in your own life, but also in the lives of others. In this way, the skills of peaceful negotiation transcend mere dispute resolution and become a true art of living.

THE ROAD TO WIN-WIN: SUCCESS STORIES

In this book, we've explored the concepts, we've taken a critical look at the principles, we've understood the ideas, but nothing speaks louder than real-life success stories. These stories are concrete proof that the win-win philosophy can be successfully put into practice.

Let's take the example of a famous natural resource conflict, the "Water War" in Bolivia in the early 2000s. A foreign company had gained exclusive control of the city of Cochabamba's water supply and raised tariffs, leading to massive protests. Instead of sticking to a zero-sum mentality, the parties managed to negotiate a win-win solution: the company reduced tariffs and invested in infrastructure, while the city's residents continued to receive water and participated in the management of the water supply.

This example shows how a seemingly insurmountable conflict was transformed into a win-win situation through cooperation and negotiation. It's a powerful reminder that even in the most difficult situations, there are opportunities to create shared value.

Another example can be found in the corporate world. In the 1980s, technology giants IBM and Microsoft entered into a partnership to develop the operating system for the IBM personal computer. Instead of competing against each other, they chose to collaborate, creating a win-win situation. IBM got the operating system it needed for its computers, while Microsoft got the opportunity to develop a product that became the industry standard.

It's crucial to remember that the success of the win-win philosophy depends not only on our ability to envisage mutually beneficial solutions, but also on our willingness to listen, understand and respect the needs and viewpoints of others.

Let's not forget the story of Rosa Parks, the black American woman who refused to give up her seat to a white passenger on a Montgomery, Alabama bus in 1955. This simple act of resistance sparked the Montgomery Bus Boycott, a civil protest campaign that lasted over a year and eventually led to a Supreme Court decision declaring segregation on public buses unconstitutional.

At first glance, this may seem like a victory for the protesters and a defeat for the city of Montgomery and the state of Alabama. However, if we take a broader perspective, we can see that it was actually a win-win situation. The demonstrators got the justice and equality to which they aspired. And although the city and state were forced to change their policies, they also benefited in the long term from the end of an unjust and unsustainable system of segregation.

These examples demonstrate the power of the win-win mentality. Whether in international conflicts or neighborhood disputes, trade negotiations or civil rights movements, adopting a mindset of cooperation and mutual respect can transform conflicts into opportunities for growth and progress.

It's not always easy to adopt a win-win mentality. It requires listening, empathy and a willingness to compromise. It requires looking beyond our own needs and desires to understand those of others. But as these stories demonstrate, the rewards are worth it.

Remember, thinking win-win means seeing life not as a competition, but as a platform for collaboration and the creation of shared value. It's understanding that true success doesn't come from winning over others, but from the ability to work with others to create a win for all. It's a habit that can transform not only our relationships, but our world. So why not start today?

HABIT #6 - SELF-DISCIPLINE: THE SECRET OF CONSISTENCY

CONSISTENCY IN EFFORT: THE KEY TO SUCCESS

If talent were the only key to success, why do so many talented people fail to achieve their goals? Why do individuals with extraordinary skills often fail in their personal and professional lives, while others, seemingly less gifted, succeed with flying colors? The answer to these questions lies in one word: consistency.

Consistency is that inner flame that drives you to get up every morning, whatever the circumstances. It's the courage to face adversity, to keep going even if the results aren't immediately apparent. Consistency is the commitment to continuous effort towards a specific goal, day after day, week after week, month after month. It's like going into automatic mode, as if you were a robot.

An oak tree grows very slowly. In the first few years, it concentrates mainly on the growth of its root system, which is not visible to the naked eye. Then it begins to grow and thicken, its trunk becoming stronger. It's a slow process, requiring a great deal of patience. Yet, as the years go by, the oak becomes a majestic, robust and resistant tree. In the same way, the consistency of our efforts may seem invisible at first, but over time it builds our character and forges our success.

Self-discipline is the driving force behind this consistency. Self-discipline is the ability to control our actions and make decisions based on what's best for us in the long term, not on what's easiest or most pleasurable in the moment. Self-discipline is the ability to resist the temptations of the moment and focus on long-term goals.

An ancient Japanese proverb says: "Patience is the key to paradise". If you want to achieve mastery in any field, you need to be patient and persistent. Raw talent is not enough. You also need discipline, patience and a constant will to learn and progress.

Take Michael Jordan, considered one of the greatest basketball players of all time. He is known not only for his incredible talent, but also for his unshakeable work ethic. Every day, he trained relentlessly, constantly pushing his limits. He was cut from his high school basketball team, he missed thousands of shots in his career, but he never stopped working hard and improving. "I can accept failure, everyone fails at something. But I can't accept not trying," he once declared. His consistency and self-discipline were the key to his extraordinary success.

Consistency and self-discipline are like muscles: the more you use them, the stronger they get. Likewise, if you don't use them, they get weaker. Successful people are those who cultivate these qualities day after day. They engage in a routine of constant effort, even when they don't feel like it. They choose to take positive action to achieve their goals, rather than letting their emotions carry them along.

What's more, consistency and self-discipline help build self-confidence. Every time you keep a commitment you've made to yourself, you boost your self-esteem. You prove to yourself that you're capable of keeping your promises and achieving what you set out to do. This gives you the strength and courage to take on greater challenges.

So how do you cultivate these qualities? There are no shortcuts, no magic secrets. It takes time, effort, and a willingness to face discomfort. It requires patience, perseverance, and a commitment to yourself.

But one thing is certain: the efforts you make today will bear fruit tomorrow. The road to success is not linear. It's strewn with obstacles and difficulties. But every step you take in the right direction, no matter how small, brings you closer to your goal.

Consistency of effort is truly the key to success. Raw talent may give you an initial advantage, but it's your ability to persevere, to stay committed to your goals, that will get you to the finish line. Success is the fruit of thousands of small actions, repeated day after day. It's the sum of all the efforts you've made, even when no one was looking.

So what are you waiting for to start building your success? Cultivate consistency, train your self-discipline, and you'll see your life transform little by little. You'll discover the incredible power of consistency, and you'll be amazed at what you're capable of achieving.

Success is not a destination, but a journey. It's the fruit of your commitment to growing, learning and improving every day. It's the reward for your dedication to consistency, self-discipline and continuous effort. And that journey begins right now, with the choice you make today.

THE PILLARS OF SELF-DISCIPLINE: STRATEGIES AND TECHNIQUES

Understanding the need for self-discipline is one thing, but how do you go from theory to practice? How can you integrate self-discipline into your daily life in a sustainable and effective way? Here, we'll explore the pillars of self-discipline and provide you with practical strategies and techniques for developing this essential skill.

The first pillar of self-discipline is clarity of purpose. To stay disciplined, you need to have a clear idea of what you want to achieve. It's not just a matter of defining vague goals like "I want to be healthier" or "I want to succeed in my job". It's necessary to define clear, measurable and achievable goals that guide you towards where you want to go (SMART goals, as we saw in Habit 1). For example, "I want to run a marathon in six months" or "I want to get a promotion before the end of the year". This gives you a clear frame of reference for assessing your progress and maintaining your motivation.

The second pillar is setting up routines. Routines are habits you establish in your daily life that help you work steadily towards your goals. For example, you could establish a running routine every morning to prepare for your marathon, or dedicate an hour each day to learning new skills for your promotion. Routines are particularly effective because they eliminate the need to constantly make decisions, which can be exhausting and lead to procrastination. With a routine, you know exactly what you need to do and when you need to do it.

The third pillar is time management. Good self-discipline means using your time wisely. This means learning to prioritize your tasks, avoid distractions and stay focused on what's really important.

Last but not least, patience. Self-discipline is a marathon, not a sprint. You won't always see immediate results, and there will be times when you're tempted to give up. But remember that success is often the result of small steps made over time. Learn to enjoy the process and celebrate each small step forward, no matter how small. Losing weight doesn't happen in 1 day or even 1 week. It's a long process that requires regular small sacrifices, but it's worth it.

Developing self-discipline involves setting clear goals, establishing routines, managing your time effectively and being patient. These pillars, once integrated into your life, will help you stay focused and motivated, even when the going gets tough. Remember that self-discipline is a skill that develops with time and practice. So don't be too hard on yourself if you stumble from time to time, the important thing is always to pick yourself up.

BUILDING A SUCCESS ROUTINE: EXERCISES AND ACTION PLANS

We've explored the importance of self-discipline and its fundamental pillars. Now it's time to take action. This subchapter is dedicated to building a success routine through concrete exercises and action plans.

We'll go over some strategies you can apply immediately to start building self-discipline into your daily life.

Exercise 1: Defining objectives

We'll start by defining your goals. Take out a sheet of paper and a pen, and write down the goals you want to achieve. Again, make sure they're specific, measurable, achievable, relevant and time-bound - the famous SMART goals. For example, instead of saying "I want to lose weight", try "I want to lose 5 kilos in 3 months". Having clear, precise goals will reinforce your motivation and commitment to achieving them.

Exercise 2: Creating routines

Then think about how you can integrate these goals into your daily routine. What specific behaviors can you adopt each day to get closer to your goals? If you want to lose weight, you could, for example, commit to exercising for 30 minutes every day, or to preparing your meals at home instead of eating out. Write these routines down and plan them into your schedule.

Exercise 3: Time management

Then try the Pomodoro technique (also seen in Habit 1) to improve your time management. Choose a task, set a timer for 25 minutes and work without interruption until the timer rings. Then take a 5-minute break before starting again. This technique can help you stay focused and avoid procrastination. Of course, it doesn't work with everything.

If you've decided to exercise for 30 minutes a day, then this method won't do you any good, but incorporate these 30 minutes into your schedule and stick to it.

Exercise 4: Practicing Patience

Finally, learn to be patient. Self-discipline is a journey, not a destination. It's important to celebrate the small victories along the way. Every day, take a moment to reflect on the progress you've made, no matter how small. This will help you stay motivated and committed.

All these exercises require practice and commitment. It's normal to encounter obstacles along the way, but don't let them discourage you. Every failure is an opportunity to learn and grow. Be patient with yourself and keep moving forward.

Self-discipline isn't always easy to develop, but it's essential to achieving success. By using these exercises and action plans, you can start building a success routine that will help you achieve your goals and live a more fulfilling life.

STORIES OF SELF-DISCIPLINE: LESSONS FROM WINNERS

Discovering how others have overcome obstacles and achieved their goals can inspire us and help us develop our own self-discipline. So, in this sub-chapter, we'll highlight two powerful stories of people who have achieved significant success thanks to their self-discipline.

Space Marathon

The first is that of NASA astronaut Scott Kelly. His mission? To spend an entire year aboard the International Space Station - a feat never before accomplished by an American astronaut. The aim was to study the long-term effects of space flight on the human body, an essential element for future Mars missions.

Living in space for an entire year requires exceptional self-discipline. Without sunrise or sunset to structure the day, and without the pleasures of life on Earth, how do you maintain motivation? Kelly developed a rigorous routine, getting up at the same time every day, devoting himself to physical exercise to counter the debilitating effects of microgravity, then moving on to his research tasks. To complement this, he cultivated stoic patience, recognizing that each day was a small step towards his goal.

Scott Kelly has succeeded in his mission, setting a new record and making an invaluable contribution to our understanding of life in space. He attributes his success to his self-discipline and ability to stay focused on his long-term goal.

The Master of Memory

The second example is Dominic O'Brien, eight-time world memory champion. O'Brien was an ordinary kid who wasn't particularly good at memorizing things. That all changed when, at the age of 30, he saw a man named Creighton Carvello memorize a 52-card deck in less than three minutes on television. Fascinated, O'Brien decided to develop his own memory.

He began by practicing for 15 minutes every day, making slow but steady progress. He practiced patience, hanging in there even when progress seemed non-existent. He used memorization techniques, creating "memory palaces" in his mind to store information. His routine was simple, but his discipline was ironclad.

After months of regular practice, O'Brien not only managed to memorize a deck of cards in under three minutes, he also broke Carvello's record. Finally, he won the World Memory Championship eight times, an achievement attributable solely to his unwavering self-discipline.

These two stories illustrate how self-discipline can help us achieve things we never thought possible. Whether it's spending a year in space or becoming a memory master, the key is to stay dedicated to our routine, be patient and focus on our end goal. Self-discipline is not a quality we have or don't have. It can be cultivated and strengthened through constant practice and commitment.

Scott Kelly's example teaches us that self-discipline can help us adapt to difficult and demanding environments, structure our time productively and stay focused on our goal, even in conditions of extreme isolation.

Dominic O'Brien's story shows us that self-discipline can enable us to develop extraordinary skills and talents, even if we're starting from scratch. It also teaches us that success isn't always quick or immediate. Sometimes it's the result of constant, determined effort, day after day, month after month, even year after year.

In conclusion, self-discipline is a powerful habit that can help us realize our dreams and reach our goals, whatever they may be. It's not always easy to maintain this discipline, but as we've seen with Scott Kelly and Dominic O'Brien, the results are well worth the effort. Self-discipline is indeed a secret of consistency, a pillar on which we can build to achieve lasting success. Whether in space, at the World Memory Championship, or in any other area of life, self-discipline can make the difference between a dream and a reality.

HABIT #7 - SHARPEN THE SAW

THE SPIRIT GARDENER: THE IMPORTANCE OF CONTINUOUS SELF-IMPROVEMENT

Visualize yourself as the gardener of your own mind. Your mind is a fertile garden that can produce wonderful flowers of knowledge, skill and wisdom, if only you take the time to cultivate and nurture it. As with any garden, if you don't keep it in good condition, the weeds of ignorance, fear and inertia can quickly take over. Herein lies the importance of continuous self-improvement.

Consider the story of Benjamin Franklin, one of the Founding Fathers of the United States. Despite being born into a poor family and receiving only two years of formal education, Franklin engaged in a process of continuous self-improvement that made him one of the most accomplished men of his time. He demonstrated intellectual curiosity, reading voraciously, learning new languages and acquiring knowledge on a wide range of subjects. Franklin also worked hard to develop his character, drawing up a list of 13 virtues (such as sincerity, frugality and industriousness) and dedicating himself each week to improving one of them. By continually cultivating his mind and striving to improve, Franklin left a lasting legacy as a politician, writer, inventor and scientist.

The lesson we learn from Franklin's story is clear: constantly investing in yourself through self-improvement is the key to achieving lasting, meaningful success. Whether you're a student, entrepreneur, artist, athlete or parent, you can always learn, grow and improve.

Self-improvement is not just about acquiring new knowledge. It also encompasses developing skills, improving behavior, reinforcing values, clarifying goals and improving mental and physical health. Like the gardener who must care for every part of his garden to ensure it flourishes, you must take care to improve every aspect of yourself to realize your potential.

So, how can you engage in a process of continuous self-improvement? Start by taking the time to reflect on your strengths and weaknesses. What are the areas in which you excel? What would you like to improve? What are your short- and long-term goals? What are the obstacles preventing you from achieving them? This kind of reflection can help you identify the areas you need to work on.

Next, seek out learning opportunities. Read books, take courses, attend conferences, watch webinars, listen to podcasts and engage in stimulating discussions. Expose yourself to a variety of ideas and opinions. Don't be afraid to step out of your comfort zone and explore new areas of knowledge.

In addition, adopt a growth mindset. As psychologist Carol Dweck has argued, those who believe they can learn and develop throughout their lives are more likely to succeed than those who think their abilities are fixed. When you face challenges or failures, see them as opportunities to learn and grow, rather than reflections of your inabilities.

Finally, remember that self-improvement is a journey, not a destination. There's no end point where you can say, "There, I've completely improved." Instead, self-improvement is an ongoing process, a perpetual effort to be the best version of yourself.

On this journey, it's important to celebrate the small victories along the way. Every book you read, every skill you acquire, every behavioral change you make, every goal you reach, every step you take towards better mental and physical health, is a victory worth celebrating. These small victories are the gems that together form the brilliant necklace of your personal development.

As the gardener of your mind, you have the power to cultivate a rich, productive and fulfilled spirit. Just as a gardener cares for each plant in his garden with love and devotion, care for your mind with the same passion. Commit to continuous self-improvement and constantly invest in yourself. You'll find it's one of the most valuable investments you can make, because if there's one thing you can't be taxed on, it's your knowledge.

THE MOTIVATION MARATHON: STAY FOCUSED ON PERSONAL GROWTH

One of the greatest challenges of personal development is staying committed over the long term. Just like a marathon runner, you need to maintain a steady pace and stay determined, even when the going gets tough. Here are a few tips to keep you motivated and focused on your personal growth.

First of all, it's essential to understand that motivation isn't something that happens to you, but something you create. While some days you'll feel naturally inspired and energized, other days will be less so. It's during these difficult moments that you'll need to tap into your reserve of determination and remind yourself why you've embarked on this journey of self-improvement.

An effective technique for staying motivated is to define clear, measurable goals. What do you want to achieve? What skills do you want to develop? What aspects of your life do you want to improve? Write these goals down and refer to them regularly. Every little step you take towards achieving them will boost your motivation.

Next, adopt the attitude of a marathon runner. Marathon runners know that to reach the finish line, they must maintain a steady pace, even if each step may seem insignificant in itself. In the same way, every book you read, every new habit you create, every new skill you acquire, is another step towards your goal of self-improvement. You may not see results immediately, but every effort counts. As the Chinese proverb says: "Even the journey of a thousand miles begins with a single step".

Also, surround yourself with people who support you in your self-improvement journey. Look for mentors, coaches, friends or colleagues who share your desire for growth. Their support, encouragement and advice can be a great help when your motivation falters.

And don't forget to reward yourself. When you reach a goal, take a moment to celebrate. It doesn't have to be anything grand; a moment of relaxation, a walk in nature or a good meal can be reward enough. These small rewards will boost your motivation and help you maintain your commitment.

Finally, feed your mind with positive, inspiring thoughts. Read inspiring books, watch motivating films, listen to stimulating speeches. Fill your mind with visions of what you can achieve and who you can become. This mental food will help you stay motivated and focused on your goals.

Think of the marathon runner once again. He doesn't focus on the pain in his muscles or the number of kilometers left to run. He focuses on the finish line, on the joy of accomplishment, on the satisfaction of having surpassed his limits. Adopt this mentality. Focus on your victories, not your challenges. Focus on what you gain, not what you sacrifice.

It's also important to maintain balance in your life. Don't neglect your health, your relationships, or your pleasures for your personal development. A balanced life is a healthy life, and a healthy life is conducive to growth and fulfillment. If you're exhausted, stressed or unhappy, you'll find it hard to improve.

PERSONAL DEVELOPMENT TOOLBOX

Any craftsman worth his salt needs a well-stocked toolbox. For self-improvement and personal development, we also need tools. These tools are not physical, but mental, emotional and behavioral. Let me introduce you to some of the most effective tools you can use in your quest for self-improvement.

- **Inspirational reading :** Surround yourself with books and articles that inspire and motivate you. These readings can offer you new perspectives, give you ideas for improving your life, and encourage you to pursue your personal development.

- **Meditation and Mindfulness:** Meditation and mindfulness can help reduce stress, improve concentration and help you to be more present and aware in your daily life. There are many online resources and apps to guide you in these practices.

- **Positive Self-Dialogue:** Your inner dialogue has a significant impact on your self-esteem, motivation and general outlook. Try replacing negative thoughts with positive, encouraging affirmations.

- **Networking and Mentoring:** Surround yourself with people who inspire and encourage you on your self-improvement journey. This can include mentors, colleagues, or support groups.

- **Continuing Education:** Never stop learning. Whether through online courses, books, webinars or conferences, constantly seek out new knowledge and skills.

- **Physical Fitness:** Your body and mind are intrinsically linked. By maintaining a regular exercise routine, you'll improve not only your physical health, but also your mental and emotional well-being.

- **Healthy nutrition:** Good nutrition is essential for maintaining your energy and concentration, which are vital for your personal growth.

- **Rest and relaxation:** Don't forget the importance of rest and relaxation. It's essential to recharge your batteries and give yourself time to reflect and integrate what you've learned.

These tools are just a few of the many available to help you on your self-improvement journey. There are no "right" or "wrong" tools; the most important thing is to find the ones that work best for you and your lifestyle. The personal development toolbox is constantly evolving, and so are you. Feel free to add, remove or modify the tools you use as you progress on your journey.

These tools are not ends in themselves, but means to help you achieve your self-improvement goals. They are there to guide you, support you, and give you the means to become the best version of yourself.

But remember: tools are only effective if you use them. Like the gardener with his shovel and seeds, it's by working the soil of our mind and sowing the seeds of change that we can hope to reap the rewards of our personal development. So take these tools and put them to good use.

FROM CATERPILLAR TO BUTTERFLY: STORIES OF TRANSFORMATION

Let me tell you the story of Jim Carrey. Before he became one of Hollywood's most famous actors, Jim Carrey was a struggling comedian, performing in Los Angeles stand-up clubs while juggling several odd jobs to support himself. But Carrey was convinced he had something unique to offer the world. He had a dream, and he was willing to do anything to make it come true. So he began to focus on self-improvement, working tirelessly on his art and on himself.

One day, he wrote a $10 million check to himself for "acting services rendered", dated Thanksgiving 1995, and kept it in his wallet. The check was a manifestation of his belief that he would one day achieve success. And he eventually did, achieving resounding success in the 1990s with films like "Ace Ventura", "The Mask" and "Dumb and Dumber". His story shows the power of self-improvement and faith in one's own abilities.

Then there's the story of J.K. Rowling, author of the Harry Potter series. Before achieving success with her book series, Rowling was going through a difficult period. She was a single mother, on welfare, and depressed. However, she used this period to concentrate on writing her book. The manuscript was rejected by several publishers before finally being accepted. The rest, as they say, is history. Today, J.K. Rowling is one of the most widely read authors in the world, and her Harry Potter series has been translated into over 70 languages.

Chris Gardner's story is another source of inspiration. His journey, immortalized in the film "The Pursuit of Happyness" starring Will Smith, tells the story of his rise from homelessness to stock market millionaire. Gardner struggled against adversity, raising his son alone while trying to find a job. Eventually, he landed an unpaid internship with a brokerage firm, which he turned into a lucrative and successful career.

These stories are testaments to the extraordinary potential that self-improvement can unlock. As the caterpillar transforms into the butterfly, these individuals have reshaped their lives, moving from darkness to light through self-improvement.

It's important to note that these individuals didn't wake up one day having succeeded. Their successes are the fruit of years of constant effort, unwavering resilience and a deep desire for self-improvement. Every day, they dedicated themselves to honing their skills, perfecting their talents and overcoming their challenges. It was a gradual process, with each small step bringing them closer to their goals.

Take Elon Musk, for example. Before becoming CEO of SpaceX and Tesla, Musk experienced a series of failures. His first rocket launches failed, and Tesla nearly went bankrupt in 2008. Yet he never gave up. Instead, he used these setbacks as opportunities to learn and grow. Today, his companies are at the forefront of their respective industries, and Musk is recognized as one of the most influential entrepreneurs of our time.

Oprah Winfrey, one of the most influential women in television history, has also had her share of hardships. Born into poverty and facing many personal challenges, Winfrey has used these experiences to forge a media empire and become a force for positive change in the world.

These stories show that no matter where you come from, no matter what difficulties you face, you have the potential to improve and succeed. Every day is a new opportunity for growth and self-improvement. Every challenge is a chance to learn and grow stronger.

Every transformation begins with a choice: the choice to believe in oneself, the choice to persevere despite obstacles, the choice to commit to self-improvement. These are the choices that make the difference between a caterpillar and a butterfly.

In conclusion, these stories of transformation are not only tales of success, but also lessons in resilience, determination and self-improvement. Whether you're an aspiring artist, a budding entrepreneur, or someone simply looking to improve your life, these stories are a reminder that self-improvement is a journey worth taking. As the saying goes, "The only thing constant in life is change." So why not turn that change into a vehicle for personal growth and development? Why not choose to become the best version of yourself? As these inspiring individuals have shown, self-improvement can take you to heights you never imagined.

THE RED THREAD: SUMMARY OF THE 7 HABITS

As we explore our potential for personal development and self-improvement, these seven habits emerge as an indispensable roadmap to guide us towards our final destination: achieving our goals and realizing our personal vision.

The first habit is to "Start with the end in sight". This involves clearly defining our goals and vision, so that we have a clear direction to work towards. It's as if we were architects of our lives, creating a detailed plan of what we want to achieve.

The second habit is "Time Management - Putting Priorities First". This habit teaches us the importance of distinguishing between what's urgent and what's important. Pareto's Law, or the 80/20 principle, applies here: 80% of our results come from 20% of our actions. So it's essential to focus on these high-impact actions and organize our time accordingly.

The third habit is to be "Proactive". Being proactive means taking the initiative and action to change our situation rather than simply reacting to events. It's like being the captain of our own ship, guiding our life in the direction we've chosen.

The fourth habit is "Seek to understand, then to be understood". This habit focuses on active listening, a powerful communication tool that promotes mutual understanding. By actively listening to others, we are able to understand their points of view and articulate our own more effectively.

The fifth habit is "Win-win thinking". This habit encourages us to seek solutions that benefit all parties involved, creating harmony in our personal and professional relationships.

The sixth habit is "Self-discipline: the secret of consistency". Self-discipline is an essential skill that ensures consistency in our efforts to achieve our goals. It enables us to maintain our motivation and stay on track for success, even in the face of challenges.

Finally, the seventh habit is "Sharpen the Saw". This habit emphasizes the importance of continuous self-improvement, as if we were gardeners of our minds, constantly cultivating and developing our skills and talents.

These seven habits are interconnected, forming a coherent system of personal development. Each reinforces the others, creating a synergistic dynamic that amplifies our growth and success.

In short, it's about adopting a clear vision (Habit #1), managing our time effectively according to that vision (Habit #2), taking initiative to achieve that vision (Habit #3), listening actively and communicating effectively to gain support from others (Habit #4), seeking win-win solutions (Habit #5), maintaining self-discipline to remain constant in our effort (Habit #6), and engaging in a process of continuous self-improvement to hone our skills and remain adaptive in the face of change (Habit #7).

This system of habits, though complex, is actually very simple when put into practice. It creates a positive feedback mechanism where each habit reinforces the others, forming a solid structure for our personal development.

Ultimately, these seven habits are more than the sum of their parts. Together, they form an integrated approach that can transform the way we see and live our lives. They are not just techniques or strategies, but fundamental principles that can guide our actions and decisions. Each habit is a piece of a larger puzzle, and when these pieces fit together, they reveal a picture of us at our best: proactive, goal-oriented, disciplined, empathetic, cooperative and committed to continuous growth and learning.

Ultimately, it's not just about acquiring new habits, it's about transforming the way we are. It's about becoming the best version of ourselves and realizing our full potential. This is the common thread that runs through these seven habits, and this is the promise they offer: the possibility of becoming the architect of our own lives and creating our own destiny.

1. THE END IN SIGHT
Visualize future success to make decisions and act in line with your long-term goals.

2. TIME MANAGEMENT
Identify and prioritize important tasks over urgent ones to maximize efficiency and productivity.

3. PROACTIVE
Take the initiative and assume responsibility for your actions to positively influence results, instead of reacting to circumstances.

4. ACTIVE LISTENING
Really listen to understand others' perspectives before trying to be understood, thus improving communication and relationships.

5. WIN-WIN
Adopt a cooperative mentality, seeking solutions that are beneficial to all parties involved, thus fostering mutual trust and respect.

6. SELF-DISCIPLINE
Cultivate perseverance and consistent effort to accomplish tasks, even in the absence of immediate motivation.

7. SHARPENING THE SAW
Invest in continuous self-improvement and personal growth to maintain and improve effectiveness over time.

BEYOND THE BOOK: CONCLUSION

Now that you've taken this journey through the seven habits, the real adventure begins. This book is not intended to be a destination, but rather a springboard to self-improvement. It's time to apply what you've learned to your own life and start forging your own path to success.

It's important to remember that personal development is not a one-off event, but an ongoing process. It's a commitment to constant learning, growth and improvement. It's not just about achieving a specific goal, but about becoming a person capable of achieving any goal you set for yourself.

So, where do you start? Sometimes the biggest challenge is taking the first step. Uncertainty, doubt and fear can prevent us from getting started. But remember, every journey begins with a single step. And that step doesn't have to be perfect. It just has to propel you forward.

Choose a habit you want to work on and make a plan to integrate it into your life. It can be as simple as taking five minutes each day to think about your goals, or setting up a morning routine to manage your time more effectively. No matter how big or small the step, the important thing is to start moving forward.

Remember, there's no secret to overnight success. It's inevitable to encounter obstacles and challenges along the way. But every failure is an opportunity to learn and grow. Every challenge is a chance to test your resilience and strengthen your determination.

The key to success is perseverance. Every day is a new opportunity to apply these habits and improve a little more. Over time, these small steps add up to big changes.

Ultimately, the purpose of this journey is not only to achieve your goals, but also to become the best version of yourself. It's a quest for growth and fulfillment, an exploration of what you can achieve when you realize your full potential.

This book is a compass to guide you, but it's up to you to make the journey. Take what you've learned here and use it to forge your own path to success.

You have the power within you to achieve anything you can imagine. All you have to do is believe in yourself, stay determined and keep moving forward, one step at a time. You are the master of your destiny. You are the architect of your future. The tools and strategies you acquire here are the bricks with which you can build the path to your dreams.

Dear reader, I encourage you to seize this opportunity. Embrace the possibility of growth and improvement. You can be more than you are today, and there's no better time to start than now.

So, take a moment to commit to this journey. Make a promise to yourself to apply the lessons you've learned and strive to be the best version of yourself. Because, in the end, the journey of self-improvement is a celebration of who you are and all you can become.

With these words, I leave you with one final thought: the road to self-improvement is never over. There will always be something new to learn, something new to discover. So keep growing, keep learning, and keep becoming the best version of yourself.

Your journey has just begun...

Give your honest opinion on Amazon!

Your suggestions and criticisms are invaluable.

They make every reading experience even more satisfying!

Thank you very much for reading my book.

I wish you all the success you deserve!

APPENDICES

Exploring Further: Additional Resources To help you dig deeper into the concepts covered in this book, here are some valuable resources I recommend:

1. **Websites**

    - **MindTools.com**: A website offering tools, resources and articles on leadership, management, communication, productivity and stress management.

    - **TED.com:** Inspiring talks by experts in various fields, including personal and professional development.

2. **Books**

    - **"Deep Work" by Cal Newport**: An in-depth exploration of focus and productivity in the world of work.

    - **Sun Tzu's "The Art of War":** an ancient Chinese military manual offering invaluable lessons on strategy and leadership.

3. **Podcasts**

    - **"The Tim Ferriss Show"**: Interviews with exceptional people from various fields who discuss their habits, routines and methods for success.

- **"Happier with Gretchen Rubin"**: Discussions on happiness, habits, and creativity to help you live a more joyful and satisfying life.

On the Shoulders of Giants : Bibliography Here are some of the many works that influenced the writing of this book:

1. **Carnegie, Dale. "How to make friends. Le Livre de Poche, 1998.**

2. **Covey, Stephen R. "The 7 Habits of Those Who Achieve Everything They Set Out To Do". J'ai Lu, 2005.**

3. **Hardy, Darren. "The Cumulative Effect." Leduc.s Éditions, 2012.**

4. **Dweck, Carol S. "Mindset: Changing The Way You think To Fulfil Your Potential". Robinson, 2017.**

Acknowledgements I would like to express my gratitude to all those who have contributed in any way to the realization of this book. To the many authors and thinkers whose ideas have shaped my vision, thank you for your wisdom and inspiration. To my family and friends for their unconditional support and invaluable advice. To my editorial team for their diligence and patience. And finally, to you, dear reader, for your curiosity and willingness to learn and grow. This book is for you.

SOURCE IMAGES

The author and publisher would particularly like to thank the following websites:

www.freepik.com

www.snl.no/

www.pixabay.com

www.pxhere.com/

www.publicdomainpictures.net

www.pixnio.com

www.lookandlearn.com

www.creazilla.com

Printed in Great Britain
by Amazon